Grassroots

POEMS BY CARL SANDBURG

Grassroots

Browndeer Press ❧ Harcourt Brace & Company ❧ SAN DIEGO NEW YORK LONDON

PAINTINGS BY WENDELL MINOR

Library of Congress Cataloging-in-Publication Data
Sandburg, Carl, 1878–1967.
Grassroots/by Carl Sandburg; illustrated by Wendell Minor.
p. cm.
"Browndeer Press."
Summary: Fourteen poems with Midwestern themes or settings.
ISBN 0-15-200082-8
1. Middle West—Juvenile poetry. 2. Children's poetry, American.
[1. Middle West—Poetry. 2. American poetry.]
I. Minor, Wendell, ill. II. Title.
PS3537.A618G73   1998
811'.52—dc20   95-46419

First edition
A C E F D B

PRINTED IN HONG KONG

The illustrations in this book were done in watercolor on illustration board.
The display type was set in Nuptial Script.
The text type was set in Kennerley.
Color separations by Bright Arts, Ltd., Hong Kong
Printed and bound by South China Printers, Hong Kong
This book was printed on totally chlorine-free Nymolla Matte Art paper.
Production supervision by Stanley Redfern and Ginger Boyer
Designed by Michael Farmer

ACKNOWLEDGMENTS

"Daybreak" from *Wind Song*: copyright © 1958, 1960 by Carl Sandburg;
copyright 1936 by Curtis Publishing Company

"Just Before April Came" and "Buffalo Dusk" from *Smoke and Steel*: copyright © 1920
by Harcourt Brace Jovanovich, Inc.; copyright © 1948 by Carl Sandburg

"The roan horse . . ." (from "Potato Blossom Songs and Jigs") and "Still Life" from *Cornhuskers*:
copyright 1918 by Holt, Rinehart and Winston, Inc.; copyright © 1946 by Carl Sandburg

"Grassroots," "Cricket March," "Summer Grass," "Timber Moon," "Crabapples," and "Man and Dog on an
Early Winter Morning" from *Good Morning, America*: copyright © 1927, 1928, 1955, 1956 by Carl Sandburg

"Six feet six was Davy Tipton . . ." (from "The People, Yes, 4") from *The People, Yes*:
copyright © 1936 by Harcourt Brace Jovanovich, Inc.; copyright © 1964 by Carl Sandburg

"Harvest" and "Metamorphosis" from *Honey and Salt*:
copyright © 1953, 1958, 1960, 1961, 1963 by Carl Sandburg

"Pearl Horizons" from *Slabs of the Sunburnt West*: copyright © 1922
by Harcourt Brace Jovanovich, Inc.; copyright © 1950 by Carl Sandburg

"Red and White" from *Harvest Poems: 1910–1960*: copyright © 1958, 1960 by Carl Sandburg

THE PAINTINGS IN THIS

BOOK ARE DEDICATED

TO ALL WHO REMEMBER

THEIR GRASSROOTS.

—W. M.

DAYBREAK

Daybreak comes first
    in thin splinters shimmering.
Neither is the day here
    nor is the night gone.
Night is getting ready to go
And Day whispers, "Soon now, soon."

The snow-piles in dark places are gone.
Pools by the railroad tracks shine clear.
The gravel of all shallow places shines.
A white pigeon reels and somersaults.

Frogs plutter and squdge—and frogs beat
        the air with a recurring thin
        steel sliver of melody.
Crows go in fives and tens; they march their
        black feathers past a blue pool; they
        celebrate an old festival.
A spider is trying his webs, a pink bug sits
        on my hand washing his forelegs.
I might ask: Who are these people?

"THE ROAN HORSE..."

*T*he roan horse is young and will learn: the roan horse buckles into harness and feels the foam on the collar at the end of a haul: the roan horse points four legs to the sky and rolls in the red clover: the roan horse has a rusty jag of hair between the ears hanging to a white star between the eyes.

GRASSROOTS

*G*rass clutches at the dark dirt with finger holds.

Let it be blue grass, barley, rye or wheat,

Let it be button weed or butter-and-eggs,

Let it be Johnny-jump-ups springing clean blue streaks.

Grassroots down under put fingers into dark dirt.

BUFFALO DUSK

*T*he buffaloes are gone.

And those who saw the buffaloes are gone.

Those who saw the buffaloes by thousands and how they pawed the
prairie sod into dust with their hoofs, their great heads down pawing
on in a great pageant of dusk,

Those who saw the buffaloes are gone.

And the buffaloes are gone.

Six feet six was Davy Tipton
and he had the proportions
as kingpin Mississippi River pilot
nearly filling the pilothouse
as he took the wheel with a laugh:
"Big rivers ought to have big men."

CRICKET MARCH

As the corn becomes higher
The one shrill of a summer cricket
Becomes two and ten
With a shrilling surer than last month.

As the banners of the corn
Come to their highest flying in the wind,
The summer crickets come to a marching army.

SUMMER GRASS

Summer grass aches and whispers.

It wants something; it calls and sings; it pours
out wishes to the overhead stars.

The rain hears; the rain answers; the rain is slow
coming; the rain wets the face of the grass.

TIMBER MOON

There is a way the moon looks into the timber at night

And tells the walnut trees secrets of silver sand—

There is a way the moon makes a lattice work

Under the leaves of the hazel bushes—

There is a way the moon understands the hoot owl

Sitting on an arm of a sugar maple throwing its

One long lonesome cry up the ladders of the moon—

There is a way the moon finds company early in the fall-time.

STILL LIFE

Cool your heels on the rail of an observation car.

Let the engineer open her up for ninety miles an hour.

Take in the prairie right and left, rolling land and new hay crops, swaths
    of new hay laid in the sun.

A gray village flecks by and the horses hitched in front of the post office
    never blink an eye.

A barnyard and fifteen Holstein cows, dabs of white on a black wall map,
    never blink an eye.
A signalman in a tower, the outpost of Kansas City, keeps his place at a
    window with the serenity of a bronze statue on a dark night when
    lovers pass whispering.

HARVEST

When the corn stands yellow in September,
A red flower ripens and shines among the stalks
And a red silk creeps among the broad ears
And tall tassels lift over all else

      and keep a singing

      to the prairies

      and the wind.

    They are the grand lone ones
    For they are never saved

      along with the corn:

      They are cut down

      and piled high

      and burned.

      Their fire

      lights the west in November.

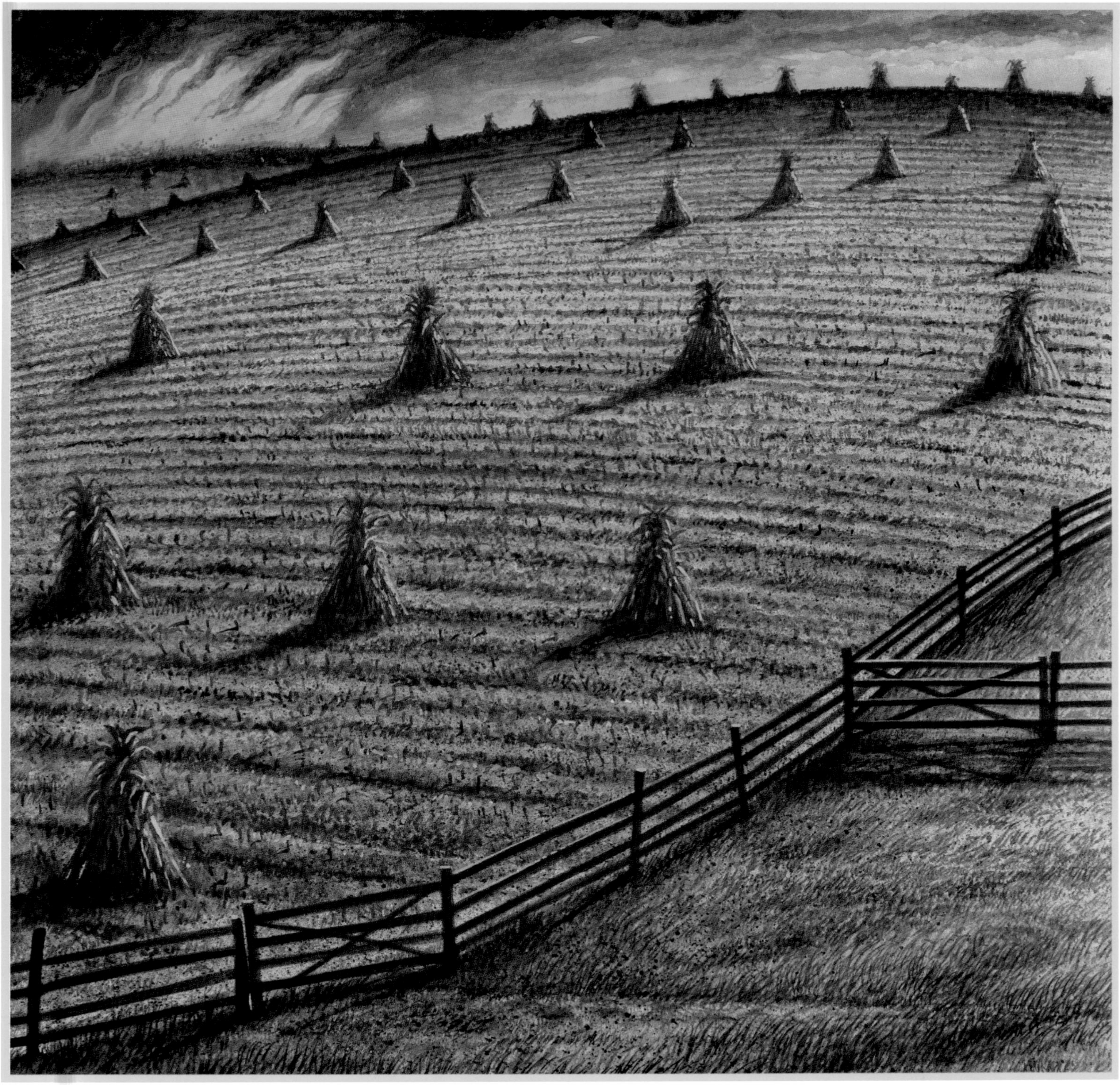

CRABAPPLES

Sweeten these bitter wild crabapples, Illinois
October sun. The roots here came from the
wilderness, came before man came here. They
are bitter as the wild is bitter.

Give these crabapples your softening gold,
October sun, go through to the white wet
seeds inside and soften them black. Make
these bitter apples sweet. They want you, sun.

The drop and the fall, the drop and the fall,
the apples leaving the branches for the black
earth under, they know you from last year,
the year before last year, October sun.

There was a tall slough grass

Too tough for the farmers to feed the cattle,

And the wind was sifting through, shaking the grass;

Each spear of grass interfered a little with the wind

And the interference sent up a soft hiss,

A mysterious little fiddler's and whistler's hiss;

And it happened all the spears together

Made a soft music in the slough grass

Too tough for the farmers to cut for fodder.

    "This is a proud place to come to

      On a winter morning, early in winter,"

    Said a hungry man, speaking to his dog,

Speaking to himself and the passing wind,

"This is a proud place to come to."

PEARL HORIZONS

*U*nder a prairie fog moon

in a circle of pearl mist horizons,

a few lonesome dogs scraping thongs,

midnight is lonely; the fog moon midnight

takes up again its even smooth November.

METAMORPHOSIS

*W*hen water turns ice does it remember
one time it was water?

When ice turns back into water does it
remember it was ice?

RED AND WHITE

Nobody picks a red rose when the winter wind howls and the
white snow blows among the fences and storm doors.
Nobody watches the dreamy sculptures of snow when the summer
roses blow red and soft in the garden yards and corners.
O I have loved red roses and O I have loved white snow—
dreamy drifts winter and summer—roses and snow.

The Gift of Grassroots

I am a son of the soil:

My mother and father were raised on Illinois farms and

told me countless stories of their rural heritage.

My childhood was filled with images of vast prairie skies,

freshly plowed earth in spring, and hot, sunny, summer

days spent on dusty farm roads lined with rows of corn.

In autumn the aroma of burning leaves filled the air, as I walked

the woods and fields with my father. We celebrated

the harvest with a visit to the county fair.

Winter brought the beauty of whiteness and bone-chilling winds.

The seasons of the heartland will be with me always.

So, too, will the beautifully descriptive words of Carl Sandburg.

Though we are of different seasons, we share a love of the land

and are bound together by our grassroots.

—WENDELL MINOR